Robin' Christmas Sing-along!

by Niki Davies

Edited by Alison Hedger

A charming new musical for Christmas which implements the National Curriculum Music Requirements

Suitable for Key Stage 1 and Lower Key Stage 2

SONGS

1. Sing, Robin, Sing
2. Rainbow Lanterns
3. Listening For Santa
4. The Marching Christmas Band
5. Flying Away (a counting song)
6. Sing-along!

A CD of the music is inside the back cover. Everything you will need for rehearsals and performances is included.

A licence should be obtained from Music Sales Limited for public performances of this work.

© Copyright 2001 Golden Apple Productions
A division of Chester Music Limited
8/9 Frith Street, London W1D 3JB

Order No. GA11220

ISBN 0-7119-8886-2

CAST LIST

Narrator(s)   *Could be an adult*

Robin

Carol Singers   *Each singer, or group of singers carry lanterns in rainbow colours*

Children   *Three to speak*

Marching Christmas Band   *Children to mime playing trumpets, trombones, tubas and piccolos*

Stars   *One to speak*

Mary

Joseph

Animals   *Single, or groups of camels, donkeys, chickens and lambs*

The number of children involved is very flexible, and the musical works equally well with "a cast of thousands" or smaller groups. Please tailor the casting to suit your needs.

ROBIN'S CHRISTMAS SING-ALONG! subdivides into manageable sections, so reducing the necessity for several all-cast rehearsals. A great help to those schools wishing to involve a large cast.

PROPS

A coloured lantern for each carol singer
A small Christmas tree
A seat for Mary
A manger holding Baby Jesus

COSTUMES

As budget and imagination allow

MUSIC CURRICULUM LINKS

ROBIN'S CHRISTMAS SING-ALONG! could be used as the foundation of a term's music curriculum. The term's work would culminate in a sparkling end-of-term show. Alternatively, just present the show as entertainment, confident in the knowledge that you are implementing National Curriculum requirements, and that the children are gaining valuable skills and understanding.

The following examples are not exhaustive, but will show how to relate the songs to the requirements.

1a: *"use their voices expressively by singing songs"*

            Each song has a different mood to encourage expressive singing.

1b: *"play tuned and untuned instruments"*

            There are lots of opportunities to use instruments. For example:

Song 3	sleigh bells
Song 4	cymbals, tambourines, woodblocks, drums etc. for the band
Song 5	instruments such as triangles, Indian bells, wind chimes, chime bars and metallophones

2a: *"create musical patterns"*

Song 6	rhythmic repetition of verse and chorus

2b: *"explore, choose and organise sounds and musical ideas"*

Song 5	related creative activity – refer to the script

3a: *"explore and express ideas . . . using movement, dance"*

Song 4	marching and actions
Song 5	dance opportunities and links with P.E. requirements

            N.B. All the songs are suitable for actions.

4b: *"how . . . dynamics can be used expressively within simple structures"*

Song 3	quiet Santa bells, getting louder as they near
Song 4	quiet band music far away, becoming louder as it nears, getting quieter as it passes by

4c: *"how sounds can be made in different ways"*

Song 6	imitation of animal sounds

5c: *"a range of live and recorded music from different times and cultures"*

Listen to a variety of Christmas carols which span many different times and cultures.
These are usually short enough for young listeners.
Play marching band music, incorporating music and movement.

OTHER CURRICULUM LINKS

Maths   Number work: **Song 5**
             Estimation: **Song 6**   estimate how many different groups are involved

English   Speaking, listening and drama.

Science   Investigative Skills: Less force = softer sounds.
                                 Hard beaters = louder and brighter sounds.
                                 Sounds of traffic and aeroplanes are quieter in the distance,
                                 but louder as they approach, and softer as they pass by and
                                 move away.

History   Discuss "morning, afternoon and evening" in **Song 1**, and the passing of time.
             Research Victorian carol singers, called waites.

Geography Compare a country village with a town.
             What would Robin expect to find in different locations?

Art   Make and colour paper/card lanterns. Discuss the colours of the rainbow, primary
             colours and mixing of colours. Talk about moods and colours.
             Create stars, big and small, perhaps using them in board games or as maths counters.

ROBIN'S CHRISTMAS SING-ALONG!

Narration   *Narrator*   (1) High up in a holly tree sat a little robin.
(2) He had a handsome red breast, silky brown wings
    and beady black eyes.
(3) There were two things that Robin liked best in all the world:
    eating worms and singing.
    He LOVED to sing!

SONG ONE   SING, ROBIN, SING

1.

Robin sings in the morning,
Loudly as can be.
Robin sings in the morning,
In his holly tree.

Chorus

Sing, Robin, sing.
Sing, Robin, sing.
Singing is better than anything.
Sing, Robin, sing.

2.

Robin sings in the afternoon,
Loudly as can be.
Robin sings in the afternoon,
In his holly tree.

Chorus

Sing, Robin, sing . . .

3.

Robin sings in the evening,
Loudly as can be.
Robin sings in the evening,
In his holly tree.

Chorus

Sing, Robin, sing.
Sing, Robin, sing.
Singing is better than anything.
Sing, Robin,
Sing, Robin, sing.

Narration

(4) Christmas Eve came, and as Robin sat in his tree he heard the lovely sound of singing. (5) Lots of people stood at the doorway of a house in the village. (6) They held lanterns and they sang and sang. They were carol singers.

SONG TWO   **RAINBOW LANTERNS**

1 Class to be

Carol singers enter in colour groups. For fewer groups use primary colours.

1. **Red lanterns, red lanterns coming up the street.**
    Here come the carol singers, this is where they meet.
    Joy to the world, joy to the world.
    Sing a song of joy to the world.

2. **Orange lanterns, orange lanterns coming up the street.**
    Here come the carol singers, this is where they meet.
    Joy to the world, joy to the world.
    Sing a song of joy to the world.

3. **Yellow lanterns, yellow lanterns coming up the street . . .**

4. **Green lanterns, green lanterns coming up the street . . .**

5. **Blue lanterns, blue lanterns coming up the street . . .**

6. **Indigo lanterns, indigo lanterns coming up the street . . .**

    7. Violet

The song pauses for the following Narration . . .(on the CD an extra 4 bar section has been added to allow for the following Narration, so ensuring the continuity of the music)

Narration   (7) Robin thought that carol singing was a nice thing to be doing, so he joined in as loudly as he could!

Robin warbles away as loudly as possible over the last verse. An ocarina or recorder could augment Robin's singing, as this must be loud!

7. **Violet lanterns, violet lanterns coming up the street . . .**

        Narration (7)   Song One Repeat.

Carol singers are dismayed and cross.

Carol Singer 1   What was that awful noise?

Carol Singer 2   It's a noisy bird in that holly tree.

Carol Singer 3   Go away! You're spoiling our carols!

Song One Repeat

7.

Narration (8) Robin flew away.

He flew and flew far from the village out into the countryside until he reached a farmhouse. He perched on a window-ledge and looked inside.

(10) He saw a beautiful Christmas tree, decorated with pretty lights.

(11) He also saw some children. They looked excited. They were listening for something.

1 Class children scene

Child 1 *ren* Listen carefully. Can you hear them yet?

Silence as children listen.

SONG THREE   LISTENING FOR SANTA

Santa Reindeers

Use sleigh bells to accompany the song.

Listen, listen, put your hand behind your ear.
Shhhh! Listen, and Santa will be here.
Chink, chink, chink in the sky,
Reindeer flying ever so high –
Listen, listen. Shhhh!

} *twice*

After the song, the sleigh bells get louder and louder, then softer and softer until the sound dies away, leaving silence.

Narration (12) Robin got very excited by hearing Santa's bells!

He jumped up and down.

He chirped and chirped, and sang and sang.

Robin Tweet, tweet. Santa's coming!
Tweet, tweet. Santa's coming!

Repeat Song (1)

Child 1 *ren or groups of* SHHH! Stop that racket!

Child 2 Be quiet Robin!

Child 3 How can we listen for Santa if you're singing?

All children SHHHHHHHHHHHHH!

Narration

⑬ Robin felt disappointed. All he wanted to do was sing for joy!

⑭ He flew away from the farm house and on to the town. Perhaps he could sing his song there. The town looked very pretty with red, blue, gold and green twinkling Christmas lights.

⑯ In the distance he could hear some wonderful music. It was a ~~brass~~ band. It got closer and closer, and louder and louder.

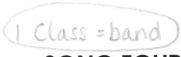
(1 Class = band)

SONG FOUR   # THE MARCHING CHRISTMAS BAND

An instrumental introduction could precede the song, with percussion instruments playing "in the distance" and gradually getting louder and louder. As each verse is sung, children make appropriate actions, as though they were playing the band instruments. Music is provided after the song for the band to get softer and softer as it gradually "moves away".

1. **Here comes the band, here comes the band,**
   Toot-toot-toot, hear the trumpets play.
   Here comes the marching Christmas band.
   Can you hear the trumpets play?

2. **Here comes the band, here comes the band,**
   Sliding, hear the trombones play.
   Here comes the marching Christmas band.
   Can you hear the trombones play?

3. **Here comes the band, here comes the band,**
   Oom-pah-pah, hear the tubas play.
   Here comes the marching Christmas band.
   Can you hear the tubas play?

4. **Here comes the band, here comes the band,**
   Trilling away, hear the piccolos play.
   Here comes the marching Christmas band.
   Can you hear the piccolos play?

5. **Here comes the band, here comes the band,**
   Playing away, hear the big band play.
   Here comes the marching Christmas band.
   Can you hear the big band play?

The following alternative words give opportunities for children to play percussion instruments, if preferred.

ring-a-ding-ding   bells

Ting-ting-ting, hear the triangle play . . .

✓

Chink-chink-chink, hear the tambourine play . . .

Tap-tap-tap, hear the woodblock play . . .

Boom-boom-boom, hear the big drum play . . .

Shaky shake shake   maracas

8

Narration   (17) Robin thought the band was wonderful. He decided to sing along.

The children repeat the last verse (unaccompanied would work best), and Robin sings over the band song.   *[handwritten: Repeat Song ①]*

Narration   (18) The band was so loud that Robin couldn't hear his own singing! He felt fed up! All he wanted to do was join in with the happy music. Sadly he flew away from the town, and found a cosy hedge by a field. He hopped inside, put his head down, and fell fast asleep. *The stars began to twinkle in the night sky.*

[handwritten left: could the band tell him to go away like others did? Yes]

[handwritten right: (19) (20) You're interrupting our song time Go away Robin]

A wind chime is played and the Stars come up to Robin's hedge.   *[handwritten: (Class = Star Scene)]*

Stars   Robin, Robin. *we* I know somewhere where you can sing.

Robin wakes up and listens.

Stars   I really do know somewhere where you can sing your heart out.

Robin   Where?

Stars *?*   *our hands we* Hold my hand and I will show you.

[handwritten right: lots of stars dance ↓ 5/10 stars song.]

SONG FIVE   FLYING AWAY
(a counting song)

More stars appear according to the counting, and join hands with Robin and the Star.

1.   **One star lights the way, one star lights the way.
We're spreading our arms and off we go,
Smile at the world far below.
We're flying and flying and flying, and flying away.**

2.   **Two stars light the way, two stars light the way . . .**

3.   **Three stars light the way, three stars light the way . . .**

4.   **Four stars . . .**

5.   **Five stars . . .**   *[handwritten: \ 10 stars]*

(With some adjustment to the script, Robin could be visited at the hedge by two stars. The counting could then be in twos, so accommodating ten stars!)

Narration   (21)   The Stars led Robin to a stable.

Mary   Hello Robin.
Can you please sing for my baby?

Joseph   This is the Baby Jesus.
He is very special.
We would like you to sing for him.

Robin   What about all the other animals?
Can they sing along with me?

All animals grunt and nod "yes".

SONG SIX   SING-ALONG!

1.   If you are a robin, you can sing along,
Join in with my Christmas song.
Sing it for the baby born today.
Tweet, tweet, tweet-i-ty, tweet.
Tweet, tweet, tweet-i-ty, tweet.

2.   If you are a camel, you can sing along,
Join in with my Christmas song.
Sing it for the baby born today.
Humph, humph, humph-e-ty, humph.
Humph, humph, humph-e-ty, humph.

3.   If you are a donkey, you can sing along,
Join in with my Christmas song.
Sing it for the baby born today.
Ee-aw, ee-aw, ee-aw, ee-aw.
Ee-aw, ee-aw, ee-aw, ee-aw.

4.   If you are a chicken, you can sing along,
Join in with my Christmas song.
Sing it for the baby born today.
Cluck, cluck, cluck-i-ty, cluck.
Cluck, cluck, cluck-i-ty, cluck.

Carol singers with their lanterns, enter during the last part of the previous verse.

5.   If you are a carol singer, you can sing along,
Join in with my Christmas song.
Sing it for the baby born today.
La, la, la-la-la, la.
La, la, la-la-la, la.

The Christmas marching band enters during the last part of the previous verse. Make appropriate actions and noises!

6.   If you are a big band, you can play along,
        Join in with my Christmas song.
        Sing it for the baby born today.
        Toot, slide, oom-pa, bang.
        Toot, slide, oom-pa, bang.

7.   If you're in the audience, you can clap along,
        Join in with my Christmas song.
        Sing it for the baby born today.
        Clap, clap, clap, clap.
        Clap, clap, clap, clap.

CODA   *Everyone sings, makes noises or claps!*

THE END

could a little more be
made of the end. It
seems a little limp.
(That this is really
special.)   ↑   I think so!

Is more needed
to pad out the story?

I'm the last to get this so I think almost
everything has been said. I agree that we
can make more of the ending. Its a shame
about the last song - the sentiments are
there - but the words at the end of the
verses/could we change them? ☺

ONE SING, ROBIN, SING

Cue: He LOVED to sing!

Sing, Rob - in, ___ sing. Sing - ing ___ is bet - ter ___ than

an - y - thing. ___ Sing, Rob - in, ___ sing.

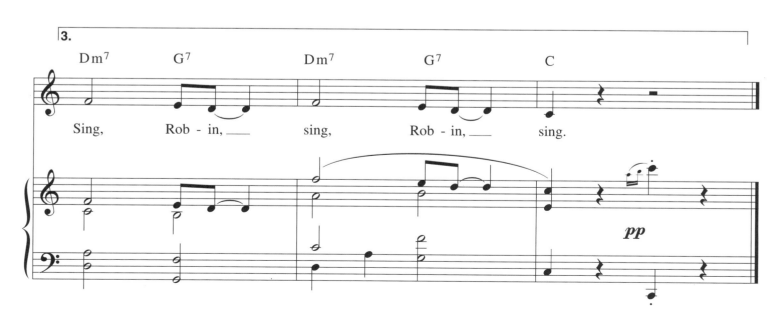

Sing, Rob - in, ___ sing, Rob - in, ___ sing.

13

TWO RAINBOW LANTERNS

Cue: They were carol singers.

1. Red lan - terns, red lan - terns com - ing up the street.

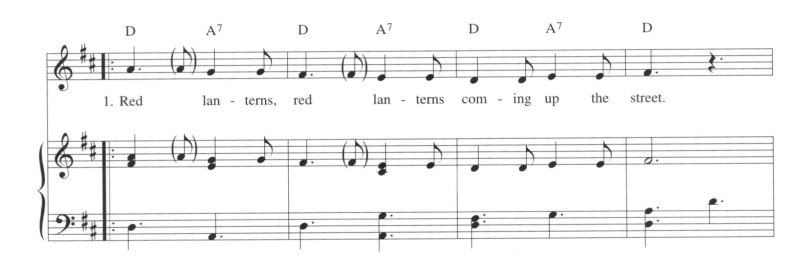

Here come the car - ol sing - ers, this is where they meet.

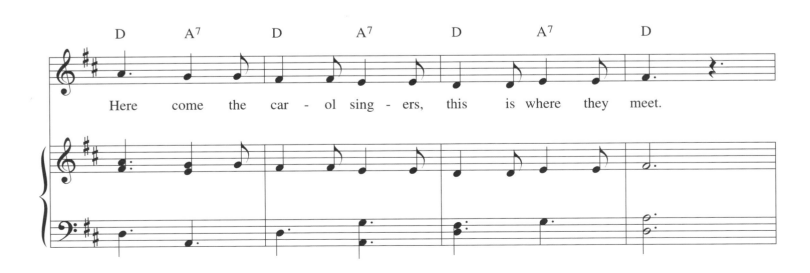

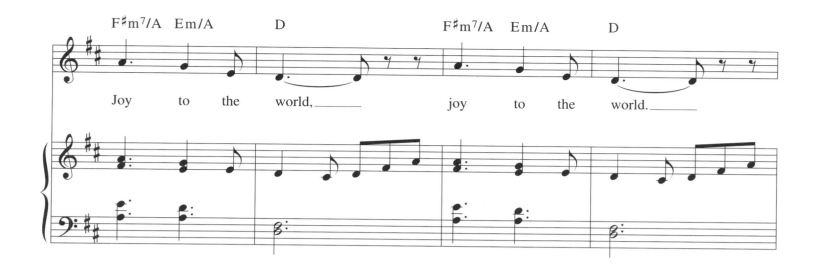

Joy to the world,_____ joy to the world._____

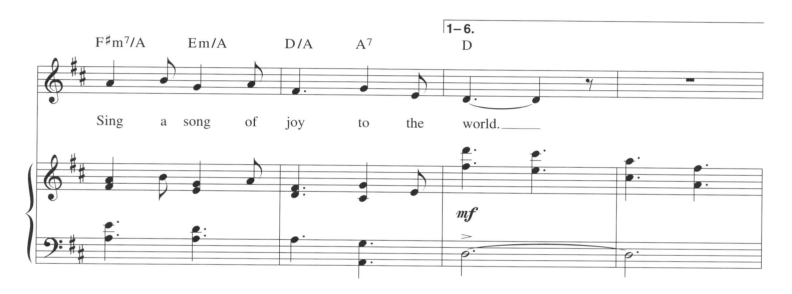

Sing a song of joy to the world._____

world.__

Verse 2 Orange lanterns

Verse 3 Yellow lanterns

Verse 4 Green lanterns

Verse 5 Blue lanterns

Verse 6 Indigo (♩♩♩) lanterns

Note: *To ensure the continuity of the music on the CD, an extra short link section has been added at this point, to allow for the narration to be spoken over the music.*

Verse 7 Violet lanterns

THREE LISTENING FOR SANTA

Cue: Listen carefully. Can you hear them yet?

Quietly expectant $\quad \downarrow = 172 \; (\downarrow = 86)$

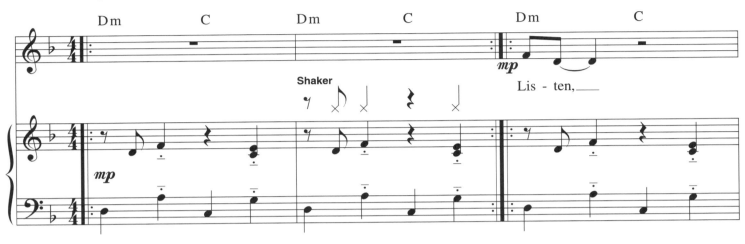

Lis - ten,___

lis - ten,___ put your hand be - hind your ear.

Shhhh! Lis - ten,___ and San - ta will be here.

Chink, chink, chink in the sky,_____ rein - deer fly - ing

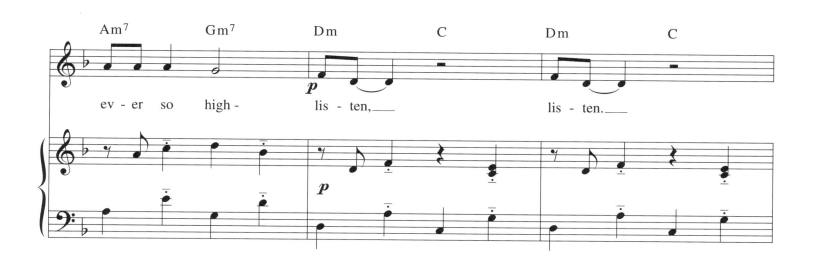

ev - er so high - lis - ten,_____ lis - ten._____

Shhhh!

Sleigh bells*

*The sleigh bells could be vocal sounds – excellent practice for volume control!

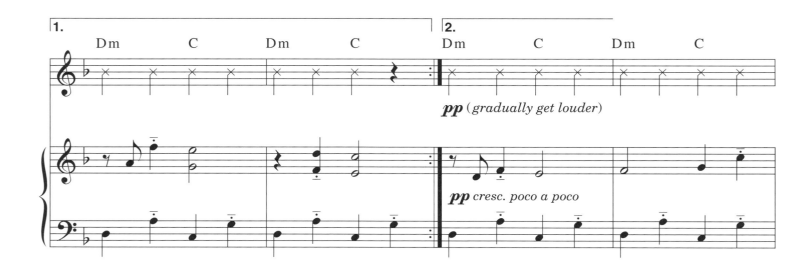

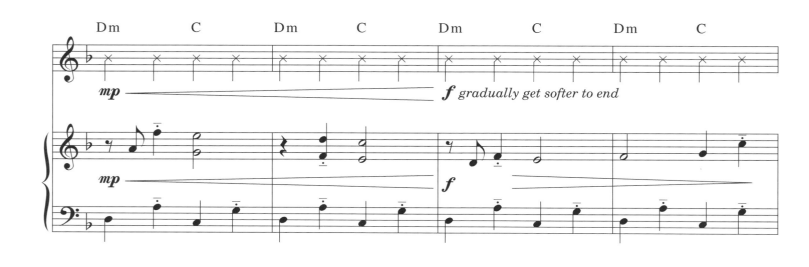

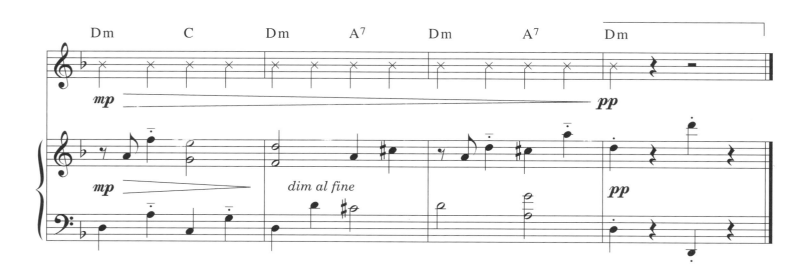

FOUR THE MARCHING CHRISTMAS BAND

Cue: It got closer and closer, and louder and louder.

FIVE **FLYING HIGH**

(a counting song)

Cue: Hold my hand and I will show you.

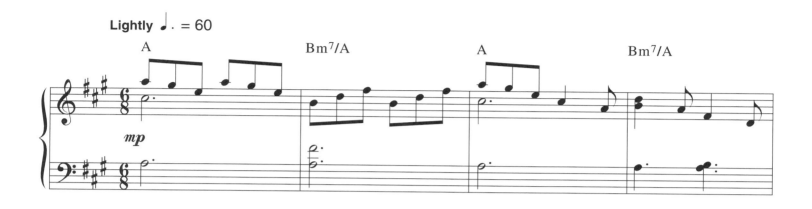

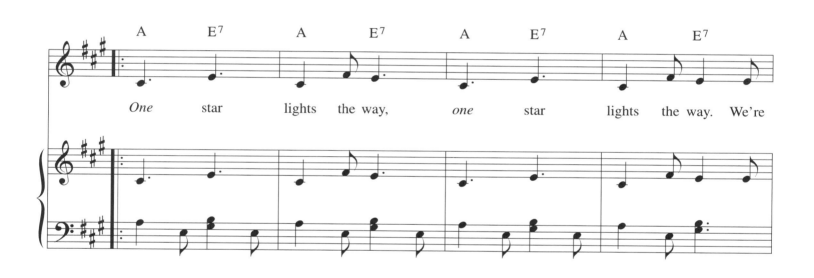

One star lights the way, *one* star lights the way. We're

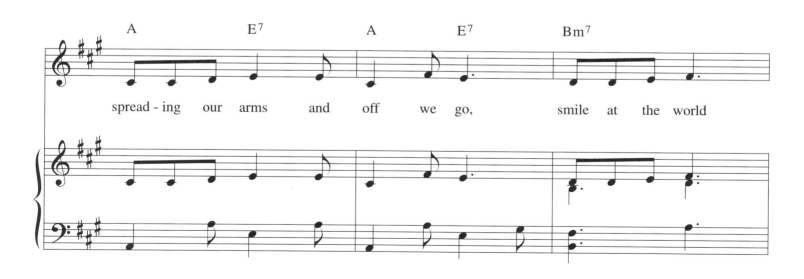

spread-ing our arms and off we go, smile at the world

far be - low. We're fly - ing and fly - ing and fly - ing, and fly - ing a -

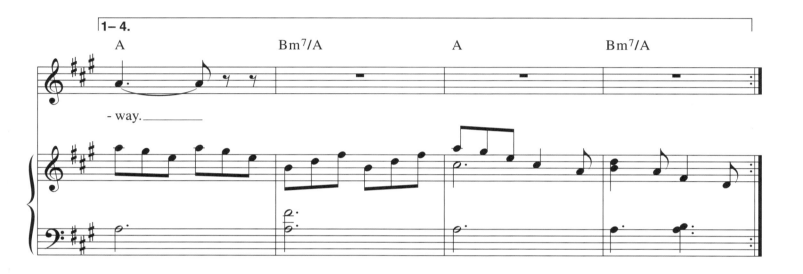

- way.

- way.

Verse 2 *Two* stars light the way . . .

Verse 3 *Three* stars light the way . . .

Verse 4 *Four* stars light the way . . .

Verse 5 *Five* stars light the way . . .

(An option is given for the counting to be in twos. See the script)

six SING-ALONG!

Cue: Can they sing along with me?

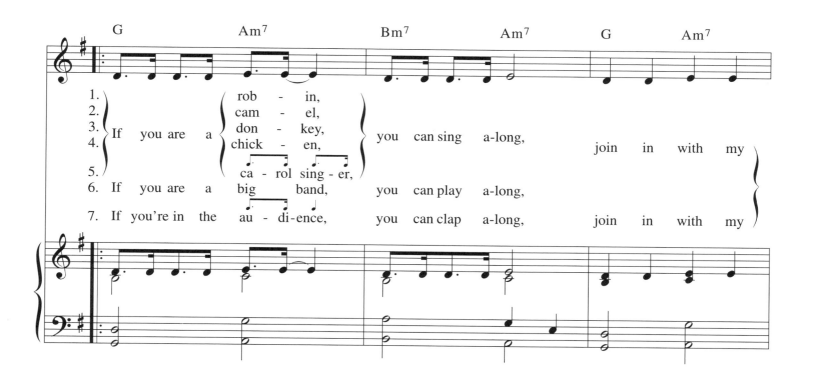

1.
2.
3. If you are a robin, you can sing a-long, join in with my
4.
5.
6. If you are a big band, you can play a-long,
7. If you're in the au-di-ence, you can clap a-long, join in with my

1. rob - in,
2. cam - el,
3. don - key,
4. chick - en,
5. ca - rol sing - er,

Christ - mas song. Sing it for the ba - by born to -